Author's Note

This little book transpired over
a period of nearly two decades.
It seems my entire life has been
a process of self-discovery.

I have always known of the angelic
realms and have sought eagerly to
be availed by natural forces. I
sincerely believe a single problem
does not come along without the
answer to its solving.

My wish is that this little book
will trigger a place in you;
will ring a voice that is your
very own and will bring you
face to face within yourself—
to you—your very best friend.

Dedication

There comes a time
when opposing forces
have to relinquish
their grip of death.
There comes a time
when fragmented dreams
sift through all opposition
and assemble themselves
on the other side.
The magical process
of spiritual thought
finding its
physical counterpart.
AN ANGEL CAME
is living proof of this.
The ones
who share these moments
with me
give power to the force
that love does
encompass all.

Contents

೮౨

Prologue

Interrupting my restless sleep
    an angel's face appeared.
I had removed myself from life
    in a small corner
        expressing and sharing
           very little of myself.
The angel asked me to relax for a moment
    her gentle eyes
        peered questioningly.
She asked me of my fears
    her heart beckoning me
        to open up to her love.
"I've been afraid," I ventured.
"Years ago I had envisioned
    a beautiful picture of my life.
I saw the wholeness of love
    my soul
        permeating the souls of others.
Life offered me to give myself.
My path has gone astray
    and remnants of memories
        are all that exist —
           memories that are penned
             in hundreds of pages."
Gather those pages and bring them to me,
    gently her voice urged.

Hesitantly I offered her my manuscript.
She then stood
    moving slowly
        and asked me to follow.
Lightly her footsteps led
    pulling me faster and faster;
        effortlessly we glided upward.
My heart became full
    and all sorrow vanished.
Love overflowed me
    my human existence became
        merely a shadow.
We must stop now, she urged.
Your earthly body
    must be viewed from here.
Your time of labor has only begun.
Curiously
    following her lead
        I turned to view the earth.
"Oh my God," I cried.
    "I see myself in everyone."
Human emotions
    intermingled in a multitude
        of colors and categories.
Joy and laughter
    pain and sorrow
        hope, despair, love and anger.
The angel sat quietly
    thumbing my manuscript.

VIII

Her eyes
  penetrating my soul.
Humans evolve, she said,
  by sharing their emotions.
Painters and musicians
  politicians and statesmen
    mothers and fathers.
All must share
  to become whole.
Tears welled in my eyes
  humanity had become a mirror.
"I've lived and experienced human emotions
  sharing only . . ."
Yes, she interrupted,
  I have shared in these pages with you.
Marking her whispered passages,
  a soft light
    emitted
      from the manuscript.
Let us return to earth now.
Promise me,
  her voice faded,
    to print, bind
      and share these pages.
In return
  I promise you —
    hearts to transform
      lives to open.
I promise you love to receive.

Suddenly I awakened.
On the night stand
	lay the manuscript.
Your hands hold
	the answer
		to my promise.

Early Whisperings

࿇

Run swiftly
the world is yours...

Sweet lover
   I stand alone
      as do we all.
Alone to be with whomever
   and whatever
      we desire.
Alone to choose
   to reckon with
      to accept and decide.
Who has the power to think my thoughts?
When has the will submitted
   without acceptance?
Happiness
   in our quest for you
      we have stumbled into ignorance,
         have protested fate,
            we've raged against
               our inner ingredients.
Yet you remain
   eternal,
      for we cannot cast aside
         the sweetness of reality.

Now perhaps it is me who is timid
   pondering alone with you
      observing your soul.
Attempting to place
   a piece of its puzzle

giving me visions of the frame
around its edges.
Allow me to work only as a catalyst.
The magic of your answer
lies in your acceptance.
The concrete facts
that your emotional nature desires
may be misunderstood
by their lack of substance.
The real responsibility
that you face
is your own independence.
A bridge has been given you
an idea for this lifetime —
the substance to remain apart
accompanied by the vision
to become involved.
Life often disconnecting that bridge
to offer standing
on the one
of your own making.

Run swiftly
the world is yours.
Cut me free
there are no
chains to my soul.
Turn it —
the key

magic filters
and uses one
as chemistry.
Straighten the house
my back door is waiting.
It was shut
until I tugged at yours
which left me standing
with mine open.

Every now and then
a special friend is made.
Every now and then
one wonders why.
Every now and then
crossroads beckon
the passerby.
And love is a has-been
a million lives before.
And love
only offers
the last waiting door.
It's funny how we surprise ourselves
the ones we love.
Quite frankly we offer ways
to bring us
closer together.
And recapping memories
takes us down

a multitude
of trails.
But I can't help but wonder
where it all fits in.
And I can't help but wonder
where we fit.
Living now
and living always
breathes inside of each other.
You offer comfort
to the spaces
I cannot fill.
In my own way of wrestling you
I give love to you
and your family
that surrounds you.
Life opens up the places
we found on the highway.
Life opens up the places
it was neither your way
nor my way.
The mountains to climb
the empty roads
to hurl down.
An open parachute
rests softly
on the ground.

Here is a gift
        you have given me.
I will change my jeans
        I will thank God
                and I will thank
                        more than that.
I will thank
        the power that
                God is
        and I will
                thank-you.

There are spots
        and there are places
                that reach out
                        to hold each other.
We have exchanged these
        and abandoned the rules.
The rules
        only make the ability
                for our own eyesight
                        to awaken.

The sweetest thing about
        the both of us
                is that we're strong enough
                        to understand each other.
There is no greater or lesser.

We exchange our
  weak spots
    for each others
      strengths.
Seek me out and come to me
  when there is no
    place of understanding.
Seek me out
  and come to me
    so I can understand why.

When your eyes
  awake from sleeping
    and your body
      may need shaving,
  I love to sit there looking.
Your burning light inside
  the night before
    my only ride.
Maybe someday
  you'll see me from a distance
    when close
      let the piece fit.
Sometimes
  shaking my head
    upsetting my bed
      keeps me well fed.
You could
  make living

                    a lifetime.
Silken
        my jungled spaces
                irregular races.
Washing on me
        like sand
                on the mouth
                        of your ocean.

Remembering your face
        the goodness
                you pour on me.
It's your simple ways
        they warm my insides
                like tea.
In the night
        I'll awake
                and think about you.
You've done something to me.
My happiness
        I want to share with you
                camp fires at night
                        running the beach
                                and laugh with you.
I've seen
        tears in your eyes
                talking to me
                        when you don't
                                understand.

19

Like an arrow
       from an archer's bow
              my thoughts are released.
Often in the hay behind
       though my aim is
              bulls-eye.
It has struck me funny
       your easy grasp on life
              side stepping
                     pain and strife.
I know there are times
       you think of my bed
              tasting my body
                     loving my head.
At its own pace
       I'll let the day by.
There is a time of day
       I ask for strength
              walking the streets
                     with you in mind.
Hoping my lucky find
       will bring me peace
              inside.

Quite slowly
       you have built
              your world around me.
Toward you
       I've done the same.

In the morning dew
    I realize
        my youthfulness.
With the passing day
    I see
        what's in store for us.
Later in the night
    on my knees
        to offer thankfulness.

I'm sitting here
    with an absolute
        clear picture
            of the love
                in your heart.
Like me
    there is an urgency
        to that picture.
A decree
    of final pieces
        to be placed.
But our picture
    for each other
        doesn't hold that.
Instead
    there is a knowingness
        I'll always be here
            for you
            and you will always

be there for me.
A knowingness
          everything that matters
                    doesn't matter.

The voice inside my heart
          asked me
                    to tell you this.
The familiar voice
          that reminds me
                    of a girl
                              who unknowingly
                                        has guided me.
Who quite frankly
          introduces me
                    to reality.
Whose spirit
          I reach for always.
Reverently and gleefully
          tomorrow
                    asks for our hand.
There is a friend
          you have hugged with
                    laughed with
                              and have asked
                                        deliverance of.
This friend
          listening to an angel's voice
                    washing your back

and your eyes
        looking into.

You'll be awakened
    early
            regardless of your late night.
You could pull
    a year or two
        of your time
            and slowly unwind.
Flying fast on a country road
    wondering about the curves
        another beer
            and dead man's nerve —
                honestly.
Whispering to me softly
    before you sleep
        your own desire
            my heart to keep.
So we can share
    I'll lay bare
        naked and open
            against the wind.
You were young
    in your own way.
You might never
    guess
        about me.

I felt
> *your spirit*
>> *coming.*

It leaped
> *out of your body*
>> *to brush my soul.*

You would never know
> *I've waited lifetimes*
>> *and not the first time*
>>> *to see your smile.*

Perhaps
> *in your busy world*
>> *I am a reflection of love.*

Untouched
> *for I've only*
>> *tasted your glance.*

The one you've shared
> *with yesterday's*
>> *lovers.*

Surrender yourself —
> *not to me.*

I'm sure you hear
> *someone calling.*

Shake yourself —
> *brush some of that dust off.*

I know
> *you're easy to live with.*

Alone in the night

dreams are shared
        willing to give yourself.
Be careful down the rapids
        the brisk waters
                may shake
                        your senses.

I turned
        and saw you
                running toward me.
I just hope you understand
        all my life
                I've been a man
                        with my
                                lovers and best friends.
You stand
        reaching for the sky.
I'm back again.
I don't know
        if this life
                will ever end.
Turn around
        and face the sun
                like we've done before.
Our wings
        are growing restless.
Let's find a place
        and let
                them soar.

You were behind me
    when I turned to catch
        your smile.
Then you led
    always knowing the direction.
My smile was strained
    my smile was a cover for tears.
You held my arm
    crossing
        the street of life.
I prayed to God for strength.
I never forgot that smile.
I never forgot the strength
    in my arm.
God knows
    I'm thankful for
        your memory
            now.

You must have asked me
    to come to you.
Perhaps you felt
    the love
        I was learning to share.
You must have
    asked me
        to come to you.
You were calling
    the way I was

reaching out
and planting seeds.
Observing no harvest.
You must have asked me
to come to you.

The inside of you
stood calling.
I know you listened.
Now opening doors
building new floors
gathering your strength
together.
Sharing yourself
is easy.
You are two
one of you
you let go
one of you
you hold close.
Life will take you
to the places
you've been waiting.
Overseas perhaps
or just distance
in your mind.
All of you
rewarded.

There is a friendship
        inside of me.
A warmth that reaches out
        to say hello.
There is a radiance
        to who you are
                a radiance that you
                        believe in.
I love you for that.
Join with me
        the thought
                of the people you love
                        protected, smiling
                                loving you.

You were a star once
        looking into
                the mirror
                        judging your body.
You were a star once
        a dark fog
                hid your brilliance.
You are
        a star now.
Nobody's
        kidding me
                about the fog.

I don't like
    walking alone
        the road
            of life.
Now it's my pleasure
    to return the joy
        the vibration of love
            you have
                sprung.

I see your face
    know your name
        ten thousand years go by.
You say what
    and how are you
        then dance without a try.
You couldn't know
    I planned
        to meet you here,
off the dirty sidewalks
    inside my heart
        I swear.
Find a dime
    when morning comes
        surprise you with hello.
I say what
    and how are you
        to whisper as I go
that's been me across the room

                    lurking in someone.
Stretching in the daytime
        darkness
                    brings my run.

Yes you —
        an everlasting fire.
Because you have burned
        because you have
                    lit others.
Fountain of youth
        glowing cheer
                    holding close
                            for many years.
Thundering horses
        your mind rages —
                    hell with the books.
You've learned with the sages.
Ever see a mongoose strike?
Susceptible eyes
        building your house
                    making your bricks
                            by hand.

You came to me
        enclosed
                in a
                        human body.

You had been looked upon
        and your frustrations
                multiplied.
You sought refuge
        friendship
                and yourself.
You gave
        and prayed
                that would not be
                        trampled upon.

Slip out of body
        lay in the air.
All
        are left to die.
Our bodies to go
        as those before.
Let your soul fill
        lifes' store.
A short time
        is all that we're here
                to either move forward
                        or fall
                                to the rear.
The ink wells are full.
The mind of the Gods
        are looking
                for someone
                        to talk through.

31

Now you loom out ahead
a thousand days
without a race.
Would complete defeat
bring you disgrace?
While Henry
put those cars together
I have a feeling
his horses
were well run.
Success is still acceptance
while the
major part's
undone.

Seems That We Know

ॐ

We could keep our smile
       perhaps
              if we were aware...

A secret from Samson
    comes whence your strength?
Silence my friend.
Knotted and braided
    then shaved his head.
Weak in the knees
    hardly lay in his bed.
A part can be given
    so much more shared.
Your soul lay open
    though hardly bared.
Fought them by hundreds
    with a jawbone of an ass

       waiting for him
            a lion in the grass.
Gates of the city
    carried on his back.
Yet
    like the rest of us
      vulnerable.
The difference between
    muscle and strength
      is vast.

You may be slow
    you may not even be started —
      make room.
Your mind is relaxed
    it has the ability to.
Come on
    don't lay back yet
      your mind is loose
        you are capable.
Yet you ask where
    you ask how
      you ask when.
Possibly
    what you believe
      becomes possible.
Possibly
    you are
      what you believe.

It's going to work with you
stand by you
and let you loose.
It comes back
when grabbed, wooed,
run after, demanded,
accepted.

We could keep our smile
perhaps
if we were aware
that a smile is linked
to the force
that can overcome and break down
more barriers preventing happiness
than all others.
Sure there is force —
why rub the grain raw
when polish
makes it smooth.

We've got our testing grounds
we choose
the grounds
on which we're tested.
Yesterday is gone
you think tomorrow maybe
you'd try again?

Longing to believe in you
     there you stand.
Hoping to work with you
     your outstretched hand.

*T*ime is precious
     indeed
              hours are diamonds.
They burn
     you know how they do.
Seems like it's fast
     seems like it's slow
              anyway you look
                   we know how they go.
So maybe
     you've felt it too
          be careful
              it creeps on you.

*S*o your way is a bit slow.
What does it matter
     about the progress?
Good folk are here
     with a little bit
          of sharing.
Were you asking too much?
Perhaps you are asking too little.
Is your giving equal to your asking?

38

Go ahead take it all
you give it all.
Everybody is looking
for a piece of you.
So you've traveled a little?
You're about getting ready
to re-sole.
A little hassle, here and there,
tell me in the morning
if the sun
doesn't shine.

Who truly knows us completely
knows what we want
how to get it
and the easiest way?
Only ourselves
individually.
Thinking is easy
thinking puts the body
into action.
Allowing no thought
we engage in
nothing.

Reaching for something
is going to keep us
going for it.

Why don't we live for something?
We see others enjoying
    the same blessings
        we're dreaming about.
Heat yourself up
    we do it regularly —
        do it now
            with purpose.
Success requires no explanations
    trying to tell us
        why you aren't winning this race.
You're talking to a deaf man.
The mirror
    offers a blind man
        to show the way.

Travels may part us
    but always
        there's a gleam.
I know you work hard
    but you got it.
Burned a few bridges
    maybe you were on one.
Know that building another
    is where your strength lies.
A piece of your mind
    has grabbed a wanderer
        sent him searching.
Now he's hoping —

yearning for his ability
to crystallize
desire.

There are a million others
hustling, laboring, looking
for something,
perhaps expression of ourselves.
Easy to see and feel
you and me
in each other.
There is an everlasting passion
seeking ourselves
and the laws
that govern us.
There have been a few
to brush against it
perhaps only look.
Yet life is waiting to
sweep us off our feet.
I believe
if you would turn around
it would be there
gazing steadily.

Take an acorn —
you tell me
how does something

that small
                become an oak tree?
With an acorn
it has no choice.
Nature has equipped it
to enable itself
to draw to it
whatever it needs.
It's going to grow
regardless.
Do you know
we are the same way?
The only difference
is we choose
whether we
grow or not.
Whatever we need
for growth and nourishment
is exactly
what we attract
to ourselves.
Once that seedling
        breaks loose and roots
                rain won't be
                        washing it away.
Dry spells
        make no difference.
It was born to win

born to accomplish.
You come back
         years later
                  and there will be a tree.
When that tree is cut
         you see the life and times
                  of that tree.
It's seen both fire and rain
         and sunny days
                  to end.
It doesn't wither and die
         all it knows is strength.
We are put here to win
         to grow
                  to accomplish.
Though many of us
         don't know
                  what we're trying to win
                           what there is to accomplish
         or anything at all
                  about growth.
We aren't trees.
We've got to decide
         for ourselves.
It's going to taste good
         but first our mouth may water
                  for sometime.
There will come a time
         we shall live
                  long past a hundred.

We will be the first to tell
how those years
were the quickest
of our life.

Into the river
a small twig did fall.
Niether did it know
whither
or how it would go.
The eager current
greeting it
only knew to swallow
it up.
The debris would add
to its
own solid banks.
The waters were calm
and the wide open space
had no chance
to cross the mind
of either one.
Basking in the current
allowing the sun
to shine its ray
onwardly it floated.
Gnashing ahead
stopped
that wide open space.

Trees that were felled
grew flowers beside its banks.
Beavers themselves
stopped hesitantly
in front of its current.
Hurried salmon were
split wide open
eager for the salt of the ocean.
That small twig
was not concerned by these facts.
The oak that born
that small twig
laughs only
at the instability
of the river.

There have been many others
by no means
you are alone.
I hope you know
a surge of power
is sharing itself
with you.
Why do you hide away?
The caterpillar
crawling among the leaves
waits happily
for its wings
to appear.

45

Late in the evening
    out in the fields
        asking questions
            common to all.
On beautiful people
    life that is full
        possibly
            never to fall.
The answer came quietly
    as life itself
        idled by.
Find something,
    the voice said,
        and be using it
            everyday.

The well is not dry
    though the cup
        must push deeper.
Some talk of pain
    or nothing is done,
        sacrificing themselves
            even their young.
May I open the gate
    without being late
        and take the road
            of joy?

All we're going to find
        is people.
Sure there is money.
It's lonely
        by yourself.
People come in masses
        and they come as individuals.
The masses are made
        by single folk.
It's absurd
        how the big cities
                are the coldest places.
Seems
        with all those folk
                they could generate
                        some love.
If not for each other
        at least for themselves.
The latter will come
        when the first
                has begun.

All I ask
        is to accept
                what is given
                        and use it.
May I see a smile?
You may thrive on fear
        perhaps sex.

Maybe boredom
envelopes you.
Do not wish
to save the world
or even change it.
Just add a little.
That little
is yourself.
I believe
in the time
you've been here
you have acquired
a certain something
that is
surely sought after.

When you are beginning to share
your face
is going to be shining;
your feet dancing.
You won't need a stage
to show
who you are.
How can you live
for one person
when so many exist?
What are you going to do
when that person's gone —
go also?

Relationships
offer pieces
to each other.
An even exchange
for the wholeness
of an individual.
Realize the blindness
giving these pieces away
with no exchange.
Relax at the longevity —
soul communication.
Completing a whole puzzle
long before
an interlocking piece
of the frame
has been
discovered.

Do you realize your luckiness?
I know we've heard it before
about the folks
in the Third World countries.
How about
the folks
among ourselves?
I eat regularly —
how can I
feel satisfied?
Do you know

where the answers lie?
Regardless of
the outside of your face
back in your head
is something.
I don't want to tread
on forbidden ground.
May I reach inside?
You've done
the same
to me.

Why does it seem
control of the mind
is the hardest task
for mankind?
Our emotions are played upon
making us creatures
of circumstance.
Willingly our minds to wander
toward
the attainment
of
nothing.

Do not say
you are not blessed
with gifts —

the ability to draw
sing
and communicate
with strangers.
Let's give of ourselves.
Where is our ear
for the folks
who have nothing to say?
Nothing to say
out of fear
no one will listen.

Does the world
owe us a living?
Certainly not.
But it is funny
how the world
will pay your living
after you have given
your fair share.
The world is
cold and unfriendly
to those
who are the same.
Turn about is fair play
there is no
other way.

Would it seem
        a soul full of love
            be lonely
                in the midst of strangers?
A soul full of love
        knows no stranger.
A stranger is a friend
        one is only yet to know.
Don't be closing your eyes.
When you do
        darkness
            is all you see.

I know the thought
        a number of stars
            live on this earth.
I've always had the feeling
        stars are in the sky
            people live here.
Open your mind
        thinking
            while growing older
                to be young again.
Somebody said
        age is like wine.
Just be careful
        which ways
            you are fermented.

I'm accepting you
        slowly.
Realizing that my life
        is not made by the toys I possess.
Power is too valuable
        to continually chase
                non-living objects.
Of course
        get comfortable.
Another is waiting
        another form of happiness
                real happiness
                        real people.
Gather the strength to carry yourself.
You could be
        subject to your emotions
                tangling with you
        getting you high
                leaving you dry
        late at night
                to wonder why.

We see the mountain
        in the distance.
On our flatland
        longing for the view.
One step
        would get us started.
One step

is all we do
at a time.
I have a tendency
to forget about today.
Why wait tomorrow
for her to turn around
and say
asking for more time
it has slipped your way.

Tasty green stuff
the dollar bill
pleasurable
to heal your ill.
Evening walking
daytime blues
ready smiling
smarts you choose.
Your friends
may be surprised
you two
were in high school.
There are instruments
of thinking
who will readily
work with you.
The law of attraction
to always be
a friend.

Thoughts set into motion
circumstances
material possessions
and personal associates.
Do understand
if one centers
their attention
on one main objective
until that objective
is realized;
that will have been the source
of its realization.

The strength I feel apart
grows together.
A little blue
put color in the sea.
The meantime
has done a lot for me.
Roll call
you're first in line.
A backroom tune
never gave it a thought
out in the wind
look how it's caught.
Money rain
morning mirror
looks the same.
Come on now

we are endless.
Heat of the pants
we aren't dogs
in the street.

Heat is all we know
where are we letting
that heat go?
Does it feel good
when it's gone
or is it gone
before it feels good?
Is there strength to know
what you are giving
is going along
not away?
Strong in the midst
of your weakness
perhaps weak
in the midst
of your strength.

Alone beside
the one
who is alone beside you.
Who knows who they are
and alone beside them
when near.

Don't be a fool
with your hurried pace
out for the ride
caught in the race.
The years stricken with tears
because somebody wasn't pulling;
that's right
pulling together.
I'm longing to run in the wind
on beaches
and lay in the sand.
The world
has been had
by a couple
a thousand two's.
Time gives one
a long day.
Deep in my heart
finding a way
to add
a little
night.

There is a freedom to life.
Survival is our game —
beyond that
we're sane.
Aloneness offers vision.
My spirits

dislike caging.
There is a hole in me
        an emptiness toward
                gain.
A mold has been offered
        to carve my tools.
I know that nothing
        can be returned
                prior to the giving.
I'll reach my arms out
        stretching
                the sun bathing me.
There is a chemistry to mind
        where we may tune in
                directly.
Our mental wavelengths
        piercing the air
                attracting
                        that which we are.

Standing alone
        love and life
                offered to no one.
Along with looking out
        comes the counterpart to see.
On the way to reaching you
        someone's gently touched on me.
You're making me smile
        you who think

                    the good lovers
                        are gone
                            or taken.
Up ahead
        that familiar song
                shall leave you mistaken.
Piecing life together
        be cautious
                with your step.
You are asking
        me to stay
                take a look
                        at things
                                your way.

Do know that it's coming
        lifes' simple expression.
Because your friendship
        is lasting
                your love
                        holds no fasting.
When the well is dry
        it is only because
                quite simply
                        you've stopped
                                digging.

*Y*our friends are off
　　with their 9 to 5.
God knows you're lucky
　　to stay alive.
The fields are waiting for your return.
Maybe this time you will learn
　　how to live and not burn,
　　　　how to grow
　　　　　　and still yearn.
I believe you.
You will strike something.
That same day
　　life
　　　　will bring
　　　　　　your own reward.

A dose of inspiration
　　being ignited at both ends.
Throw the wheat into the wind
　　let the chaff blow.
The struggling inside
　　one day may cease.
After the love has gathered
　　look about
　　　　see the tools which are used.
Sharpen them —
　　not a hoe or a shovel
　　　　your love.
Seek the night air

realize
        your youth.
The universe
    is longing
        to use
            a suspecting soul.

The beauty that lies in humanity
        has grabbed our heartstrings
            pulling gently
        enabling us to draw from the well
            of refinement.
The arts, theater and music
        remain virtually untouched.
What has been mistaken for madness
        is nothing other
            than a release of passion
                expressing life's own existence.
Gnawing pain for some
        others endless joy.
But for all
        reaching and pulling
            longing to release inhibitions
        to bridge the gap of communication —
            soul talk.

Our relentless passion of soul
        woe to those

                    whose channels are dammed
                        or surging
                            without direction.
Life is change —
        may it be toward beauty?
Must solitude
        be dull and uninteresting?
The joy of struggle?
Strength is gathered
        one becoming strong
            by lifting weights.
Our world of directing thought processes
        towards pushing out
            attempting the unknown.
Reaching inside for health, wealth
        demanding that goals be attained.
You said that it was easy —
        I don't believe you.
Hindering growth, binding chains
        to the creative nature
            physically debasing mind and body
                consciously attempting daily
                    suicide;
        living life with the evils of destruction.
Friend on earth
        that is what's hard
            continual hatred
                habitual groanings.
I do believe you
        for it is easy —

that is to smile
and to love
to care for
and share with.

Turn my back
walk away.
Love the morning
start the day.
Life becomes
the connection.
Your moments of arrival.
Be careful of that wandering
the intention of your mind
has been taken
rather damned
seriously.

What is that magnetism
that gives one
incredible possession
over circumstances
material objects
individuals
and those at mass?
The ones
who love you
and are your least concern.

Your attention
is on somebody
whose least concern
is you.

As the laborer in the field
we too
should be a steady job.
Enjoy the challenge
falling backward
may be part of
forward travel.
Let those times be few.
Never knew the answer
life exchanged for dreams
it may be
just that.

Your eyes are looking a certain way
and a certain way
has stepped up to greet you.
You're smiling
because you know certain laws.
You know how to give to get
and you know that giving
is getting.
Come back to yourself
when you're with somebody

and then you're with somebody
and again somebody.
The whole time
you are somebody.

Raw and natural
the ability
to work with
is here.
Will must be added.
Seems you're right on the fence
learn what to do.
Long before the morning
it had seemed very cold.
All of your time
was not bought or sold.
Someone
left it up to
you.

May I Taste You
from a Distance?

❧

I'm asking for your wisdom
very quietly...

Darkness will come
    slowly
            amidst the trees.
The moon
    I feel her rising.
I wonder if she showers
    ready for the night.

It will be a long one
        lovers tangling
                a thousand entertainers
                        for it's Friday.
Maybe I can start anew
        with fresh ideas
                forgetting I've dreamed.
The dangers of memories
        and a thousand falls
                all night walking
                        the empty halls.
Strung out hope
        that wore thin.
Forget that now
        and just begin.

Some folks will bring a smile
        others just a stare
                sometimes your insides
                        start raising my hair.
Hot pants
        find someone to get into.
There are a thousand ways
        that is
                to feel.
One time without a touch —
        how come you're asking so much?
Tomorrow
        never comes.

We had better start living.
A lone boy is
        asking for your vision
                asking for your strength
                        willing for some wisdom
                                to be washed
                                        upon the banks.

Would the other side
        be different?
The limo to be washed
        the dock and the yacht.
Of course darling
        the clothes are beautiful.
I saw you in the forest
        clearing the snow
                for a place to sleep.
Railroad bum
        breaking the window
                seeking refuge from the cold.
Days passed in hunger.
Behind the fog
        lay the sun
                its shine only blocked
                        not nearly gone.
A stranger at dawn
        greets the morning
                alone in his mind
                        realizing the warning.

71

Brushing the dust off his knees
         crying to the sky —
                 please.
How lucky they say
         and naturally gifted.
Strength from inside
         is your own salt
                 sifted.

It is a pleasure
         seeing you here.
I am awkward with the flesh.
It strikes me
         the feeling of lateness
                 my friends waiting patiently
                         to explore.
I'm tired of pushing
         soul has something in it
                 that requires pull.
If my insides
         would lead
                 the decisions that trouble me
                         would clear
                                 naturally.

Back again
         to touch your hand.
Thank-you.

I grasp slowly
　　the things I can handle.
There have been others
　　standing back
　　　　working for forces
　　　　　　to envelope them.
I'll work with you
　　I have now for years.
A smile from you
　　since you're leading.
You know what direction
　　most of the struggle has gone.
Shortly now is dawn
　　unloosen my soul
　　　　let it travel
　　　　　　let it go.
Uncage my mind
　　wisely handle
　　　　space and time
　　　　　　always seems to comfort me —
　　　　　　　　dreams.

I know you dream
　　of things
　　　　that are

　　　　　　apart
　　　　　　　　from you.
Alone at night
　　building pictures

in your mind.
Your flight has been delayed.
Perhaps
    your wings
        have not grown.
Pulling at my insides
    I will not believe
        any other way.
Tomorrow is
    awaiting our grasp.
A calmness
    comes over me
        for in the morning
            I shall see
                your face.

Holding me
    the swirls in my mind
        losing consciousness.
Calling my name
    as if I were a newcomer.
Sweeping me up
    a helpless babe.
Turning my head
    allowing me to see
        with my harsh words
            and unpleasant ways.
It's funny
    how you forgive.

I promise you
    if you were to jump
        you would not fall.
When you do stand
    it's rather tall.
Don't be alarmed by your animal nature.
If you would
    share some of that heat
        in a rather discreet
            way.

They're asking you
    to pull out
        stand up
            and be somebody.
Don't let them down
    all they expect
        is you.
Not what
    you have been
        or what you're going to be
            but what you are —
                and that is
                    beautiful.
When you were setting your price
    did you realize
        the sacrifice?
Oh, they would be calling.
In the meantime

you'd better accept
a small change.
A day at a time
let's not
let them
slip by.

The heat
I long to share
quietly
builds in my mind.
I'm at a loss sometimes
wondering
where to offer oneself.
Outside my door
life calls to me.
Like a man
high on the roof
sometimes
I fear
the jump.
I admire
those who have gone
before me.
The day will come
I'll be standing
on the other side.
Unaware
still pushing on.

I've got room in my eye
        for a
                very small tear.
One
        that would trickle
                slowly.
Just enough
        to where I can taste
                the salt.
I've seen that same tear
        not one
                but in floods.
Those that
        Olympic gold medalists share
                Grammy award winners
                        Presidential elections
                                and Miss America.
There is a special pride
        in reaching out,
                a special pride in achievement.
I held my hands out
        for warmth and love
                the return has been
                        ten thousand fold.

I feel you touching me
        again.
Not physically
        the way you did

when I was younger
            before my seeds had been sown.
Haunting me
        in my expression
                of life.
You had done it to others
        those
                who would let you.
Fooling us
        perhaps
                into believing ourselves.
Life would be our friend
        our joy spells
                never end.
Oh you're a sly one
        you hadn't warned of the
                hardship.
Yet you led us to believe
        it would
                only make one stronger.
Now
        I offer thanks.
Perhaps because it's spring
        and my own seeds
                have sprouted.

I'm asking for your wisdom
        very quietly.
I know that no one can hear.

You've probably grown
        quite accustomed to me.
The guy in back
        standing
                while the others are
                        seated.
Feeling
        the inside of their heads,
                making
                        the outside of their beds.
Somedays I feel your acceptance.
You will bring me
        the changes I've worked for.
New inspiration
        I must be fed daily.
I'll offer myself to the wind
        in hopes she'll send
                a broken heart to mend.
Let sleep hit my eyes
        then you wake me
                with your surprise.

Let me drift away
        into the minds
                of the friends
                        I don't know.
My spirit
        to travel and share.
Build me from inside

wrestle with me.
Give me strength
to overcome.

It seems funny now
years later
how the soul
remains
untouched.
I've seen you
looking in the mirror
impressed by your
handsomeness.
Would you wait
a lifetime
before standing?
In your own way
love has
touched you
not left you.
Open your mind
I still catch that
feeling of small.
Feelings
those of dreams untouched.
There is a loneliness
in the night
for accomplishment —
our ability to win.

Is life searching you
finding a piece
of its existence
in your solitude?
Turn your head slowly
sudden movements
are blinding.
A mature willingness may follow.
Your soul shines
its blues and greys
are melting
my stubborness.

Watching the sun go down
nothing more than
hanging around.
Sleep some of the day
making time to lay
familiar streets
more than what the eye meets.
There is gold out there.
A simple place
is awaiting
our arrival.
Using our head
to get
the lead
out of our pants.
Still I find

working saves the day.
Once you set
     your sights in the sky;
          better make a way
               to get there.
I know
     and you know
          making excuses
               gives one
                    slow go.

You bring peace
     to me.
There are fragments
     of thought
          that I have
               sewn together.
A quilt warming
     our earth.
I am eager for more thread
     many of you
          and all colors.
Hold on to the thought
     of sharing
          and make this
               a patchwork
                    of love.

You hardly know a thing
    yet you are eager.
All school is not recess
        the bell has rung,
            on your desk is a pen and pad.
You would not
    compete against
        everyone.
Your own soul is pushing you.
Forget the others
    let them
        do what they like.
Find yourself.
Your stoned accent
    must your eyes
        always be sunken?
It would be easy
    would be
        so damned easy.

Just 'cause
    you were back there smiling.
I never was good at nothing.
You pulled something out of me.
Alone on the street
    change is available.
Who is that boy?
Do I recognize him?
Not you.

What are the reasons?
Love.
Love of you
 love of money.
Giving aid.
I mean the changes
 the real ones.
Tired of
 no tracks
  this —
 what have you been doing lately?
Old buddies
 no need to wonder.
Maybe the love of a woman
 maybe
  just the belief.

I notice the sun
 has you
  in its rays.
You cannot find a better spot
 to spend your days.
Lover of life
 watching passer-bys.
Grasping your soul
 while the pain
  inside
   dies.
Laborers

in the field;
buildings under construction.
Junkies on the sidelines
go down in their destruction.
Life being given
life being taken.
In its own little corners
the world has been shaken.
Banks hold our money
lovers share our honey
and eternally we live
or so it seems.

If I may
silently
offer thanks.
The full moon
raging sea
desired ingredients
remain inside me.
Have your cake
and eat it too.
Bake your cake
then get full.
I could live differently tomorrow
to think of all
the times
I've tried.
Unbroken promises

we have no whispered lies.
Sometimes I go
        unnoticed
                as a stranger.
Yet I'm here
        lurking
                demanding
                        of myself.

Quietly making my way
        thinking of
                those of you
                        like me.
Where each day
        offers a way
                for paving our street.
Your friends
        want to know
                how have you been.
It feels so good
        to see them again.
And where have you spent your time?
I know it's your heart
        ready to start
                and never let go.
You may be alone
        yet you
                quietly
                        blend with the crowd.

There's a friend of mine
        who comes out in the eve
                after the sun
                        has decided to rest.
Her spot in the sky
        the night to herself
                quietly giving her best.
Season to season
        regardless of blues
                without any reason
                        is she paying dues?
Overtime
        the days grow long.
Patiently shining
        throughout the night-long.
The secrets she holds
        encompass the earth.
Long after I die
        way before birth.
As I run through the night
        quite willing you see
                to give up the fight
                        for her shine on me.

You've noticed in the morning
        the sun coming up.
Flaming beauty
        bringing light to the earth.
I wonder this morning

if it's thinking of me.
If I asked it
        it would give strength to me
                or just heat and light
                        to help me see.
The moon in her coldness
        offered nothing.
I dare not ask the stars.
I'd rather be here
        talking to you.
You who are real
        you who long to feel.
If I can
        have you
                my next meal
                        I will.

The years won't stop now
        I hope you have accepted them.
The vehicle
        that you've chosen
                to guide you through them,
                        is it satisfying you?
I wonder if you feel the need
        to relax on your speed
                for one loving deed.
In your younger days
        you were taken behind the barn
                and beaten like a horse.

Something in between
    then and now
        has slightly changed my course.
Thank you.
School doesn't fill your days
    no job
        holds your restless ways.
Yet you cry to me
    of your labor.
I think you've got it made.
Something simple
    has pounded your brain.
Now your life's a movie screen.
For one moment
    turn the projector
        off.
The stillness of the air
    is shaken
        by your own vibrations
            coming toward you.

Piece of quiet
    where an assembling
        of the soul
            takes place.
There has been a yearning
    toward gain.
Monetarily, spiritually, absolutely . . .
    you could say this to me.

Help me in my decision.
I've put the numbers
        out too far.
Let me awake
        and be
                at zero.
A starting point
        to observe, enjoy
                where my plan is reality.

One more boyish face
        gave way to shaving.
My friends
        I'm thinking of you
                gathered around
                        scraping together
                                bread
                                        for more high.
Good looking bodies
        exploring each other
                temporarily.
Never doubt power
        ability for success.
The rules have been laid
        like simple addition.
Years have been spent
        laying ground work.
An explosion
        preparing itself.

My basic structure
    of life
            does me.
Yet I am
    the maker of the plans.
A spider
    on float
            leaving my silk behind.
Constructing a home life
    to enjoy
        my meals.
I've got plans on surprising you.
My meat hungry days
    stalking for pleasure
            remain.
You had better be careful —
    your trigger finger.
Buckshot of mind
    does have
            a rather startling
                impact.

If you will carry me
        into the wind
            the places
                    I will never be.
You're there
    to turn to
            like the others have.

I know I'm prodding
        I'll continue.
Simmering heat
        turned loose on the street;
                the wisdom to know
                        the willingness to act.
The places to go
        when to
                turn my back.
The elevator
        has stopped on the second story —
                walk it.

There is peace
        beauty
                where we find it.
Whispering winds
        an unused skill
                forgotten trade.
You still are listening.

Stand up to me —
        allow
                my inner being
                        production.
The soul of me strength
        my weak links
                replaced.

An iceberg
      the whole of me
            submerged.

Develop a little patience
      let a seed grow.
You might want to get up and travel some.
All this time walking
      something says run.
Alive and healthy
      green and wealthy.
You may have to pay some
      lay down your gun
            empty the bullets.
Stepping slowly
      halfway holy
            I had been beckoned.
Do enter in
      surprise me,
            I heard her sweetly.
Let me turn my face
      the back of me
            has been
                  browned.

You could find a new way
      you had those times before.
Maybe paddle once again

you're so damn near the shore.
Heat
        expressed from below,
                someone to taste your meat
                        please don't come
                                to go.
I heard somebody asking
        now it's up to you,
                share yourself with everyone
                        or just a few
                                will do.
When I turn
        why don't you
                jump me
                        and wrap your legs around.

If ever I forgot
        to tell you
                I love you
        I'm not forgetting
                now.
If ever I forgot
        the heat that swallows me
                your memory reminds me
                        somehow.
And so I travel the road
        where you have been.
And so I travel the road
        reaching out again.

There is hope
        you have given me.
I reached out through you
        and to you
                for me.
You never waivered
        at your own conviction.
You hesitantly shared
        in places
                that were not comfortable.
All of life is given to you.
All of the life you share
        becomes you.

Out of the Garden

❧

Your sweet scent
      is that how nature does it...

I woke up early
        the road called.
I wondered if I was
        making footsteps
            or following tracks.
Relentlessly the trail
        prompted me.
Nowhere the road led —
        nowhere is all I said.
Hark — embark
        a ridge ahead
            a place to peer out of.
Open highways
        beg aggression.

Thought pattern of peace.
Quietly singing
    while passing
        a slow moving vehicle.
Nobody was ever me
    yet that is me —
        the slow moving vehicle.

There is a new place waiting.
I feel your body tugging
    your soul
        may easily uncage.
Calling for you.
God that music's
    still there.
Pull on me again
    the way you used to.
Lay on your back with your eyes closed.
I'll never do you harm
    my face will disappear
        yet my spirit inside
            will reach you.

That feeling of pull
    spirit being lifted
        from body.
Out to mingle
    the roads
        have got my footprints.

Don't think you run alone
	hiding from the mobs
		forget the ringing phone
			side stepping the fools.
Change your mind
	I only wish you would
		give your insides.
We naturally could
	pull together
		live forever.
I know you want heart
	that's
		one hell of a start.
Erase my memories
	years without stand.
Call me again
	my outstretched hand.

It seems
	before the last piece is fit
		almost finished
			better not quit.
A little more sure of your ways
	your wasted nights and days
		are productive.
Asking to be a magic man
	you see no reason now
		dreaming what you can
			somehow

is working.
I always knew
    summer would bring it
        the coldness out of the folk
           who crawl away.
Pry the inside of our world open
    and share with others.
It's not against the law
    you know
        to do those things
         that is
           love a little.

You made up your mind
    to spend a little time.
The return may surprise you.
Now I'm ready for some meat.
I'm smart enough to know
    it's me alone
        who buys and sells.
You wouldn't be wise to follow?
Perhaps so
    paving your own way
        let's go.

I bet you're strong enough
    to carry that load.
Take care of yourself

the kids too.
You sit back
    and live
        the quiet life.
Quiet
    is fine
        yet the inside of you
           should be spilled.

Remembering the days
    struggling
        a boy pushing weight
           hoping for strength.
Quietly waiting
    and dawn
        love her rays
           wash on me.
It's funny how we believe
    in love
        to heal our wounds.
Law and order
    please be true
        my natural wish
           friends with you.
Soaking my head
    with herbs and healing spices
        mixing together
           a potion
               of power.

Somewhere in the darkness
you lie waiting
eyes glowing
blood raging
amidst your veins.

In the years of searching
perhaps something
had dawned.

There is peace
to being alone.
There is a need
beyond that
of physical.

Night time
lays with its thighs spread
morning comes to search another.
Strange heat in the night
would not fill
my emptiness.
There is something pleasant
years of loving
still feel more
your smile
an open door.

The evening
to accept my kiss
then again
at dawn.

Alone for a cup of tea
        left over stone
                prodding my mind
                        the same story.
Early dawn
        the strength you give
                lies unmatched.
I'd never ask but a smile
        the kind you might share for good
                or pass me by.
The outside is flesh
        good meat
                is easy to find.
A little soul
            I'll share.

Thank-you for accepting me
        the times like now.
I'm a little out of reach
        escaping reality
                to enjoy my own fantasies.
It would be an ideal situation
        living daily
                practicing and enjoying
                        ones awareness.
I do it on purpose
        get out of touch.
My sensual background
        is rather dated —

yet my continual stubbornness
  asking for your wine
    my portable chair
      to dine.
It's a habit I've fallen into.
My shaken days
  have been traded
    my loosened ways
      quite honestly shaded.
I wonder about tomorrow.
Seems I could hurtle myself
  into the time zone
    I desire.

Mother of the sky
  there are things
    I must know.
Must it take
  a lifetime
    of being
      on the go?
A slight smile in your eyes
  you've heard
    the children's cries.
You have felt
  the hunger too
    seems the pain
      would make you blue.
Careless laughter

in the room
slowly bringing
life to ruin.

Your whisperings
made me think
about a lot of things.
You reminded me
all things worth having
are worth going for.
You insisted
no matter how far I go away
I am loved by more life
than I know exists.
You remembered me saying
that love pursues
and gains its own understanding —
something about
hope
is the undertaking
of our own measure.
I call to your understanding
all that you reminded me of
exists in you.

It is rather easy
for my head
to turn away.

I'm molded
     and appear sometimes
          as stone.
Glancing back on my day
     the little way
          you struck my attention.
Coming at me
     warmly.
I may brush you for awhile.
Still I feel
     I'd rather know you
          this way,
     where it's easy for us
          to be friends.
My nights
     aren't for
          my days to mend.

You will be loving somebody
     thinking you are
          then knowing
               you aren't loving them;
     you are loving
          who you want them to be.
People are who they are
     not who they've been
          not who they want to be —
               who they are.
The love you are giving somebody

is the same love
you will give somebody else.

Maybe to taste everyone
there is no need
how about a few —
those who long for you.
An untouched heart would soon turn stone.
If we were alone
it would be understood;
but there are thousands,
thousands who want to give.
Life is a two lane highway
and there you are —
a one way street.
Why not submit our passions?
There are hungry souls
our release
would be their fill.
We want a fair exchange?
Let's not forget to give.
Mingle ourselves
folks are real
images
just dance upon the mind.
Flesh and blood
there are
no exceptions.

It's going to take a lot of strength
　　to keep your head.
You will be waking up to yourself
　　no matter who you are sleeping with.
You'll have your times
　　alone
　　　　in the midst of everybody;
　　　　　your love gone
　　　　　　　along with your lover.

Stand up
　　nobody will be putting you down.
Your head won't drop
　　until you let go.
When you do
　　all you lose
　　　　is yourself.
I know who you are
　　and you are
　　　　everything
　　　　　　you've got.

Are we being hung
　　by the rope
　　　　we've made ourselves?
On fire from inside
　　out of reach
　　　　upon our shelves.
A crime against us
　　could be

        our jealous hearts.
Love
        turning fury
                raging from all sides.
Vicious mind games
        do more
                than hurt our pride.
Our small world
        is changing —
                we'd better
                        keep abreast.

So you did
        reach out a bit.
The red in your cheeks
        embarrassment.
I may think of another to win
        it would surely begin —
                a smile
                        for years.
The ability to change
        your jeans.
Remembering your teens
        when you could wear
                the same ones.

I'd like to leave you alone
        a small spell.

What the hell —
      we may both find
            a better way
                  for spending time.
I don't mean
      off in the distance
            or running
                  around with your friends.
Something's
      deep in my mind;
            I'll be awhile
                  before
                        my uprooting ends.
You've asked me for this.
I'll need your help
      my feet
            don't beg to leave.

I'll search the night
      looking for you.
Your whisperings to bring me
      to your door.
You seem
      careless in your thoughts
            concerning
                  my time.
Perhaps it's my friendship
      you enjoy
            talking to you

offering myself
    to you.
But I'm wearing you thin
    my life's yet to begin.
Instead of kissing your cheek
    I may just laugh at you.
But you'll have me
    the inside of my heart
        out to you.

Strike out anew —
    the passer-bys would not care.
Something's deep inside
    now it's time to share.
Sweet sweat
    from early summer
        those sighs come late at night.
Relentless disappointments
    now strength is gone
        to fight.
Little darling
    it's been a long time.
How come it seems to be
    the savage fury in your eyes
        is lashing out at me?
I'll love you
    because I've always loved you;
        I just don't want
            to love you close.

It's only fear
        that keeps
                us apart.
We dodge
        to run the other way.
It's only fear
        that keeps us
                silent.
Your shadow
        doesn't elude me.
It blends easily
        in my
                darkness.

The hollow stare
        you gave.
Waiting
        those empty spaces
                to be filled
                        by me.
Remember when
        stepping through the glass
                your reflection
                        smiled?
A picture
        of yourself
                may lead you
                        to crawl in.

Wrestling in the night time
    now you've got me running.
I sat looking at you.
You may wonder too.
I've felt this need before.
Down the city sidewalks
    running with me.
Depths of life
    hell to fight —
        grabbing reins of hope.
Man of my word
    nobody heard.
I don't mind
    whatever time
        against the wall
            my back will do.

It may not have been
    a good idea
        to lay open —
            vulnerable.
I never thought my heart would heal.
Walking in the darkness
    there have been
        a few high bridges
            calling to be
                friend.
It doesn't seem these days
    I'm showing off that side of me.

Unlike riding a horse
        getting bucked off
                and jumping back on.

My heart reached out to you.
My footsteps never had the courage to follow.
Instead I walked the streets
        for hours in the rain.
I learned a lot about life.
I watched myself go out on a limb
        for people who carefully
                secure themselves
                        while sawing it off.
I watched myself give everything away
        concerned about the needs of others.
The only friend I saw
        was me
                blinking my way
                        through the rain in the streets
                        and you.

There is a guy I know
        I saw him today in the mirror.
"Be my friend," he said;
        "there are others you will know
                others you will love.
The pain in your heart can be used
        as seed for a new joy.

Don't fall for the old trick —
        that of
              hardening the heart
                    being hurt
        and then stepping upon others."
There are many toys to play with
        motorcycles
              fast cars
                    and stereo systems.
I never put my heart
        in this category.

I've talked to you
        still I wonder
              if you know.
It's my own success
        I'm after.
And so we love
        as people do
              outreaching and forlorn.
You've touched with no return.
It's me I'm talking to
        yet you're standing here.

I've got to choose
        another game
              where winning
                    is the option.

My option.
I might like
standing alone
beside you
enjoying.

Lovers you have tangled with
friends you have known
high places you have been to
depths to be thrown.
Through the haze
I feel your gaze
longing of soul.
Mass of maze
unending craze
where to go.
Your straight line
sorting the highs
and down days.
The endless nights
ungoverned ways.
Do know the changes
bringing wisdom to mind.
Do know your spirit unbound
by space and time.
My whole life
spent growing up
though I've been shaving
for years.

The inner ability
        to bridge the spaces —
                desire versus reality.
The framework of my being
        a skeleton of thought;
                intermingling
                        struggle and joy.
Ride with me on the waves.
The essence of your being
        pulls at me
                longingly.
You could be reaching
        you could be calling
                hope to God
        you know where your strength is.
Silently sidestep
        negative pull.
I know you're eager —
        no
                means fool.

Working
        might have put
                callouses on our hands.
Kind of proud
        for the way
                our house stands.
The car runs great
        it's just that

the tire is flat.
Funny the wonder
    of a small change.
Maybe
    you were somebody's
        counterpart.
Perhaps you'd better
    look in your heart.

The inside of you
    is being pulled.
Has someone grabbed you
    leaving you helpless
        for their manipulation?
You had offered
    your soul
        to the wind.
You had given your love
    to friends.
The mellowness you felt
    yesterday
        must be replaced
            by new seed.

I sense your values may have changed
    in a position
        where strength is needed.
A wolf

in sheep's clothing
             the surprise upon waking me.
You must have shaken yourself
       while leaving.
A thought scares me
       one of blind reason.
Lift yourself some —
       don't forget
             tomorrow's on its way.
Reckless pleasure
       scars along the way.

As a snake
       on its belly
             let me change skins.
The soul of me
       offers a way
             to move gracefully.
Yet the awkwardness
       as my body fumbles.
There are no laws
       against uselessness.
Man to emphasize
       fashion news and political trivia.
Yet who are we
       unaware
             ignorance does carry
                   a heavy tax.

You may have taken me lightly
        standing outside your door.
Asked me to wine and dine
        lay upon your floor.
My back was turned
        as it will
                always be.
The other side
        I'm looking at
                I fear you'll never see.
Innocent bystander
        why wait for lines of old —
                warm days in the sun
                        at night you're looking cold.
Better grab yourself a seat
        the bus is filling up
                fill your stomach
                        find a place to stash your cup.
Instead you're walking
        quite alone
                as nightfall greets the street
                just to yank your head around
                        to whomever
                                you may meet.

It's generally distance of mind
        I'm after.
There are ways for making progress.
I remain caught in the conflict

             desire — vs — reality.
A friend was saying
      how the years pass.
I'd rather not look at the years
      life must be measured
             in change.
Building a puzzle
      choosing the pieces.
It's surprising
      the unexpected
             our hopes and plans
                   mean nothing.
Life barges
      not always kindly.
I must have been
      asleep
             at the bus stop.
It seems to be my shadow
      flagging
             for the driver.

Run from how you feel.
Forgetting the doors
      spoils and whores.
The sun asks for our hand.
It could be days
      before I give again.
Soul slightly tried.
If I could

step aside
            and do it again.
I do daily.
Change me
      part of you is well seasoned.
The soul of me needs salting.
Fresh kill
      I could steal of you
            for meal.

There is no way of knowing
      why things so abruptly
            happen the way they do.
A whirlwind of questions
      that have no answers
            will haunt you.
My heart soars in thankfulness
      by the presence
            of your spirit and body
                  intact.
Always know
      there is a greater God
            and a greater good.
Each experience
      no matter how meaningless
            and sometimes cruel
                  prepares us
                        for greater lessons.
Don't for a moment

relinquish
your ableness.
Lifes' whisper
can easily be heard
by the stark reality
of its
extinction.

There's been times
shared by all
in driving rain
about to fall.
Banging your head
with nothing instead
your own
empty sound.
Let your knees
drop quietly to the earth
remembering
you've been here
since birth
alive.

The soul
of one
had burnt.
The ashes
spice

            building flavor.
In ones ignorance
        to believe
                the stream
                        had been crossed.
All rivers
        lead
                to the mouth
                        of the ocean.

Every now and then
        I must turn and face
                the wall of water
                        crashing down on me.
Every now and then
        I question
                the friends
                        I gather around me.
Every now and then
        I cry
                and wonder why
                        I'm so alone.
Every now and then
        my friends reach out
                to lead me home.

I fell subject
        to my wanderings.

Life's tasteless desires
    I could not
        get my fill.
In the morning
    when I awake
        I may catch a glimpse
           of your face.
My head will turn.
At a snail's pace
    I have grown
        ready wings
           remain unflown.
Now I'm reaching
    out to you
        that's what love is for.
My ears go deaf
    to hear the sound
        please don't reach
           no more.

Smoky cardrooms
    bare assed dancers,
        endless hustlers.
You make a dime
    and they
        make a nickel
           off that.
Walking the malls
    browsing the bookstores.

Finding comfort
    where
        and with what you can.
Wrestling
    bloody well fighting.
A bruised conscious
    separate corners —
        battered subconscious.
Yet you remain vulnerable
    somebody somewhere.
A grain of sand
    blade of grass.
While mind is a monster —
    a million watts
        meat
            and flesh frame.
Oh the darkness
    fumbling
        for the switch.

I'd never believe it
    years ago
        my plans would be useless.
A problem arises
    from
        living for tomorrow —
          blindness sets in.
Wishing ahead
    is a strange sort of life.

Living behind —
    an open door for strife.
When there's desire to learn
    the part that burns
        creates growth.
I've gone out of my way
    to put my back
        against the wall.
A beautiful picture
    is
        picking up after the fall.

I used to think
    it took blood and guts.
It wouldn't bother me
    regardless how much.
Cashier
    in the sky
        keys still ringing
            adding my total.
What strikes me funny
    the ability to see.
How come
    can't we be
        all that we hope for
            maybe more?
I don't like that feeling
    of falling.
I'd rather go uphill

            crawling.
We learned
        before we could talk
                watched the others
                        though we couldn't walk.
Someone said there is fate
        I'm making mine.
Otherwise
        I would have missed the mine
                much more
                        the shovel
                                to dig.

Our time may move
        a little faster.
Something we have waited for.
You hadn't wished to get heavy
        just a simple way
                to express feelings.
Filling our cart with apples
        the ones at the bottom
                may spoil.
Use ourselves wisely
        a bit of satisfaction
                from a days toil.
We stood wishing for the sun.
Now that
        it has
                broken through —

tan.
I've always believed in patience.
Now she's hurrying me
        outside my broken window
                calling me
                        to see.

Another Sunday
        followed
                by the driving passion
                        to remain.
You would never guess
        my fear
                of losing you.
I would if I could
        turn my head.
Early Sunday morn
        for this day
                I was born.

When the slowness
        hits you
                alone on the street.
Thinking of your lover
        and dreams
                miles away.
Still
        that small turn of events

could uproot your existence.
The leather on your coat
        is wearing.
Your shoes
        much too thin
                for the months
                        you've had them.
Singing the blues
        with no song at all.
Burning inside
        to jump for the call.
Touch your hair
        kiss your feet
                talk with folks
                        yet to meet.
Still you hang on —
        falling
                would get you
                        nowhere.

I should pass
        on
                an easy way
                        to forget the urgency.
Long days of stillness
        foresee the storm.
Slow days in the sun
        make yesterdays.
Hardcore strain

blued out vein
        does the same.
Then the helplessness
    a calf in the herd.
Victim of rustlers
        getting skinned
            for the meat.

Evening hours
    assembling the master plan.
Morning
    brings the rug
        pulled out from under you.
Misfortune
    has certainly employed allies
        who thrive on overtime.
It's not a pleasant scene
    losing the leg
        to the chair you're sitting on.
Nature has devised
    a rather abrupt way for testing.
Allowing
    us
            to build our blocks
                to scatter them
                    with her wind.
Jokingly to whisper —
    time now
        to begin.

I have seen you stronger
    pulling together your forces
        eternally you remain willing.
Come to the realness in life.
Leave the images
    in your mind
        alone.
You have put yourself
    a little out of reach
        sliding slowly.
Grab the slack in the rope
    a little spark to your hope.
Your world is
    piecing itself together.
Don't hurry me
    down the road.
Realize
    I feel the earth
        beneath my feet.
You would feel more comfortable
    closing in.
Your mind is
    a willing servant.
Send it out for a loaf of bread
    to later reply
        that's all you said.

As a bull
    led by a nose ring

                    my own stupidity
                            embarrassing.
Coming at me
        dirty water
                barging lifes gutter.
Oh God in heaven
        the sun is
                peeking at me.
Don't you ever doubt it.
It has busted up in laughter
        observing our games
                the rituals we play
                        in our search
                                for sensual pleasure.

I'd like to
        forget the meat
                beautiful bodies.
Hell with this
        fantasy from a distance.
Even though
        I seem trained
                my eye
                        that of a hawk
                                piercing
                                        devouring the flesh.
At night walking peacefully
        exercising mind.
While day —

damn it
　　on the prowl
　　　　exchanging glances.
Want to
　　jump you
　　　　without a word.
Leave you still
　　unheard.

From a distance
　　smell
　　　　the honey.
These broken blues
　　worn out shoes
　　　　still paying dues.
You like being down
　　comfortable
　　　　on the ground?
I don't believe you.
Yet our helplessness
　　to match the skies.
It ain't funny
　　how time flies
　　　　away.

You think I'm a fool
　　when you've got me
　　　　like this

                on my knees?
Give me regular hassle
        instead of
                inside turmoil.
May I water the land
        instead of
                digging the soil?
Nature
        I can hardly call you my friend
                as you continually
                        spit at me.

I haven't seen tears
        for years
                now they're welling in my eyes.
No one heard the laughter
        why should someone
                hear the cries?
With our struggle inside
        seems our face would hold
                a hundred lines.
Ten times that
        for all the countless times
                we've tried
                        and fell —
                                flat ass fell.

They left you
      on the edge of the wall
            just to see
                  which way you'd fall.
Twisting your arm
      listening your call
            taking notes on your passion.
Had you noticed them
      the good and the evil
            grabbing for you?
Longing to feel
      plastic faces
            mistaken for real.
Just wanted love
      long to give my share.
Peace of a dove
      show me you care.
Those bricks he's building —
      flatten them.
You think you can go on forever?
After a thousand times down
      hardly ever
            a day goes by
                  that I won't stand
                        to challenge you.

I heard you calling
      though my head didn't turn.
Upstairs

itchin' with yearn.
Now I'm longing for miles to part us.
I've seen you for years
        a natural care.
Lifes loving game
        all's fair.
You may never see inside.
White heat
        maybe just died.
No.
Loving souls longing
        loving souls belonging
                to no one.
Morning mist
        encircle me
                with the pleasure of freedom.
Let the miles come and go
        let the smiles easily flow.
A couple years
        could not
                separate a passion.

Your sweet scent
        is that how nature does it
                enough to bring
                        the dogs out of the woods?
I was there
        in back.
All of us together

a running pack:
Spitting fire
    your wonders to amaze us.
Drawing our heat.
I forgive easily
    you too are vulnerable.
Sobbing on your knees
    your make believe plans
        begging me
            please.
Oh you're a hard one.
Your savage eyes
    leave me gasping.
Your silken lies
    have me grasping.
I'd rather pass.

In the leaves you lay
    coiled and tense
        as a rattler.
My barefoot strides
    were graceful
        without pain.
I could have dodged
    the venom
        of your strike.
The heat
    that rang through my body.
Running wildly

searching high places
to throw myself
off of.
Yet deeper
below the surface
a calm began.
The sweetness in your fluids
is not poison.
Now wringing my hands
searching a towel.
Master Craftsman
the clay
needs molding.

OutBack Insides

ꕔ

Always always always
a still voice beckons…

There is an electrical
    current
        that surges
            a place for all.
There is a heart beat
    a place to rest
        next to.
There is
    a turning
        point.

In the quiet afternoon
    I saw

somebody whispering to me.
Hearing those voices call
what on earth
could it be?
In the murky gloom
I was gathered up
and bound tightly.
The subject
hadn't struck me lightly.
A day or two
no difference it made.
Hot and thirsty
calling for shade.
Now they're running
oh God
I see them.
Please turn around
someone unbind me.
In the darkness
my eyes opened slowly.
Something gathered around me
so holy.
Hands were sweating
limp at my sides.
Until then
I hadn't realized.
The girls on Fourth Street
still sellin' leg.
The hungry children
oh mama

they beg.
Rock 'n roll
        from music stands.
Red Cross
        and helping hands.
Suddenly
        I felt useless —
                caught in the mass
                        with my little
                                working world.
How slow my time unfolds.
I could not live forever.
If I have 'till now
        I hadn't known.
Love and peace together
        sprouting seeds
                that I had sown.
Yet I could not
        console myself.
I knew that I must
        try again.

Always always always
        a still voice beckons.
A sound ringing
        with all parts intact.
We interrupt that voice
        and fumble endlessly
                in the confines of a body.

We would shake all of heaven
        and have plunged
                the fiery depths of hell.
The sound of the voice
        prompts us
                and elusively
                        it remains.
Times own essence
        invites us
                to inhabit
                        the ring of that sound.
To act and embody
        the stillness
                of that voice.
To release
        the structural confines
                and leave them
                        to our own
                                bidding.

*Earthly traveler
        art thou ready
                to awaken from thy slumber?
Has the eternal searching
        for empty pleasures
                left you wanting?
I have watched
        over your years
                of abandonment.*

Won't thou
        allow my blessings
                for your sight?
Make peace
        with your heart.
Let go
        of the images
                that bind one
                        in ignorance.
As the snowfall brings whiteness
        to the blackened crusts
                of your earth
                        let my love
                                purify the darkness
                                        of your heart.

Is not it easier
        to walk smiling
                to the gates of your father
        than wretchedly weigh upon
                the paths of damnation?

Slumbering into sleep
        knocking at lifes' door
                teaming up with age old souls.
Receiving guidance
        through inspired channels
                of allowing
                        inner workings of thought.
Opening lines of communication

and sharing our presence.
Realizing an urgency
a need to discover
a dormant
yet enlightened
humanity.
Facing the challenge
of bringing the whole
of earth
to the opening of
heaven's gate.
Traveling without hesitation
for the unification
of love.
Knowing our only burden
is the withdrawal
of the work.

Mother Nature
gasped in pain —
struggling to retain her soul
fighting conditions
reducing her to a
worthless slave.
Trampled now
by the birthing experience
of mankind.
"Forgive me the years,"
she pleaded.

"Knocking endlessly
        on the closed door
            of your heart.
My thoughtlessness
        ignoring
            the answer of your silence."
Echoing in the darkness
        our eternal soul
            I Am.
Feeding fire to the rage inside
        searching those
            who will assist.
"Must you throw yourself away
        does your inner voice
            stop
                    at the growl
                        of your stomach?
The meek to inherit the earth —
        the whole group of you
            to fertilize it."
For new life to be born
        death is inevitable.
For the earth to house
        sovereign whole individuals
            man's dependencies must die.
Offer a new way
        where housing, food
            and communication
                no longer aborts nature.
We have no place to hide —

who of us
will search inside?

There is a quietness
to the soul of the earth.
A quietness
thundering
in the hearts of her listeners.
A peacefulness
torn and shredded
by the ragings
of our cruelties.
Her workings go unnoticed
only by those laughing
in the folly
of their blindness.
Please work with me.
Let us quicken the lengths
of her footsteps
journeying homeward
to the outreached arms
of our father.

Surveying the pages of history
observing our hope for the future
one thing becomes evidently clear
we have underestimated loves' simplicity.
Without scholarly reason

and scientific investigation
        I venture to say
relationships
        are our
                single most important
                        ingredient.
Time has come to recognize
        each other
                as ourselves.
Don't misunderstand my individualism
        understand
                gathering together
                        the whole.
Our human rate of evolution
        depends distinctly upon
                the acceptance of each other.
How can we continue
                the eternal separations
                        of human embodiments?
The strength of a chain
        is measured
                by its weakest link.
I understand reincarnation
        I understand
                Adam and Eve in the Garden;
                        and 'space brothers'
                                are my best friends.
What I don't understand
        is us —
                and by no means

upperclass
in this galaxy.
There are a thousand complicated theories
a thousand ways
to transcend.
I don't think
any one of them
holds a candle
to old fashioned love.
We have our ways
of enhancing ability —
our crystals, mantras
and astrology.
We study our chakras
and surround ourselves
with white light.
I think we forget
the open void
can be traced directly
to love.
I am as romantic as the next guy
but the only thing
I see derived
from the
Adam and Eve story
is an excuse to blame
ones weakness
upon another.
Any fool can see
if man was built so God holy

                    he would not have fallen
                        for Eve's line.
I am damned upset
        by generations of unequality
            cultures
                    built upon these standards.
Who's kidding who —
        the most able vessel
            would be chosen
                        for the birthing
                            of a species.
We'd better bring
        'Peace on Earth'
            a little closer to home.
Taking individualism and freedom
        from women
                is a crime against nature
                    a crime
                        we are paying for dearly.
For God's sake
        when I marry another
            she doesn't become me
                neither do we become one.
Oneness
        is grossly interpreted as
            one sidedness.
Living together
        working together
            and lovingly
                supporting each other

brings strength and unity.
If there is any oneness
　　　it is the oneness
　　　　　of becoming a whole individual
　　　encouraging another to do the same.
Opposites attract
　　　goes beyond the field of magnetics.
The laws of nature
　　　do not mold
　　　　　opposite polarities
　　　　　　into one.
Let us come to grips with reality
　　　our little working world
　　　　　makes for a much larger whole.
We are not victims of circumstance —
　　　we are circumstance.
We are not different from each other
　　　the air we breathe
　　　　　is the recycled pantings
　　　　　　of another.
The birthing process and bodily functions
　　　know no
　　　　　foreign policy.
The animal world
　　　flocks together, herds together
　　　　　and runs in packs.
A little human intelligence
　　　would allow us the same privilege.
A lot of human compassion
　　　would insure that.

The evolutionary rate of science
        moves us on.
Our great accomplishments
        more accurately stated
                are an eternal destruction
                        of nature.
We are on the
        endangered species list.
My friend
        that is what we are
                species.
Man —
        created in the image of God?
Whoever inspired that statement
        had better back-up and regroup.
God's image
        is all forms of life.
Life that breathes
        feeds, mates, and pushes forward.
Life that was here
        long before us.
Life that would rather we go.
I think the dolphins
        and a thousand other
                peace-loving animals
                        more reflect the image of God.
If God is a predator
        God is
                conquering all that is encompassed.
If man is created in God's image

God is no more or less
             than a great white shark.
God is the government
       that killed the Indians,
                buffalo and wolves.
God is the oil
       in the Middle East.
'In God We Trust'
       that is rather touching.
I wonder if the billions of dollars
       spent yearly
                for the military
       would be a more accurate means
                of measuring trust.
My long thread of incarnations
       like yours
                are either coming up for air
                       or going down
                              into the sea.
It's going to take
       more than this little candle
              to combat the weather
                       we have gotten ourselves
                              into.
I am helpless
       observing the planet
              helpless
       hearing the cry of hungry children.
I am angry
       because I can hardly feel the pain.

My screamings and shoutings
        intermingles
                dead bodies
                        maimed landscapes
                                and history books.
I am embarrassed —
        the air I breathe
                is taxed by
                        my own stupidity.

The structural foundation
        of bloodstained religion
                flinches
                        at the steadiness
                                of Loves' gaze.
Hatred and evil,
        permeates its auric field.
Scribbled are names, dates
        and signatures of stubbornness.
"I'm curious," Love ventures,
        "you the maker of Gods
                with your face of stone
                        and lines hardened
                                by discontent.
Surely you are not ignorant
        to your greed and ruthless prey
                sucking the life
                        of the youth.
Carnivorous cannibals

continually conniving
        convincing cowards
                to compile convicts.
Masters of cunning deceit
        beguiling believers
                baiting them
                        as a fish hook.
Wretchedness
        has washed on you
                tears of anguish
                        you have bathed in.
It is your own sins
        you wish to have balanced.
One cannot mirror
        in anothers soul
                the plight of their own grievance."
Love breathes for a moment
        willing as a channel
                to contact
                        the structural foundation
                                of bloodstained religion,
        willing to transmute
                dull sunken eyes
                        painfully attached to limbs
                                that ache beyond the sense
        of their own instinctive survival.
Love knows
        that every marred piece of history
                every division of humanity
                        every caste system

and place of submission
        has the ability
                to open its heart
                    and allow
                            the onslaught of goodness
                                to flicker brazenly.
The ability
        to accept each other
            as human beings.
Human beings
        born into a world of pain.
Human beings
        born into a world of endless hunger.
Individuals
        facing a mirror
                that no crimson robe
                    or burning stake
                        can alter.
A mirror
        that the Papal crown
                or the snapped neck
                    on a hangman's noose
                        will not tarnish.
Eyes in that mirror
        that peer back questioningly
                haunting ones own
                    instinctive survival.
Eyes in that mirror
        attached to a body
                that ticks steadily

toward the open arms
of death.
Nature is neither partial
to the begat
or the begotten
the become
or the became of.
All share the same oxygen
all inhale
the excess
of another's breath.
Love breathes again for a moment
a twinkle in her eye
a knowingness
that all must die.
A willingness to surrender
and let the goodness
of its own essence
trample ties
that bind all
in slavery.

*If there is a torch you must carry
or a cause you must rally about,
open both eyes
and see the inner workings
of a structure
before blindly
slinging mud at it.*

Be aware when supporting a peer
the ignorance of their mouth
reflects upon you also.

When blubbering and baying as hounds,
the trap in the forest
cares not which foot
steps upon it.

Progress in this world is not achieved
by belittling those
who leave tracks for us to follow.
Many uneventful lives
encompass biting
at the heels of another.

Rewards come through initiating
and pioneering projects.
Fools are easily spotted giving advice
on things they know little
or nothing about.

Befriend the stranger in your mirror
for the answers in life
you will need.

The most precious life force today
        are the children of this planet.
It is plain to see
        survival is distinctly related
                to our offspring.
If children inherit and pursue
        the destructive tendencies
                handed down through generations
        the modern day war machine
                will eliminate
                        all life
                                in one gasping breath.
Rapid advancement of technology
        is but a mirror
                of a child's formulative stage.
There are people alive today
        older than the first plane in the sky.
The most precious life force today
        are the children on this planet.
We must accept
        a peace-loving generation.
We must allow
        the shattering
                of the war-hero image.
Bring an end to
        the fashionable trend
                of fighting a blood thirsty,
        second-hand coward's battle.
We must accept a peace-loving generation
        or we must accept

                    death.
Barriers
        those of
                race, color and creed
                        disease
                                a child's mind.
Barriers
        those of
                race, color and creed
                        are demanded
                                by adults.
Let the eternal circle of the earth
        introduce our children
                before hatred
                        has a chance to.

There is love
        you express.
Always asking peace
        for your off-spring.
There is love
        you have shared with others,
                others who have tasted your smile —
                        the hope your eyes have
                                shined forth.
You have reached many
        and it is my pleasure
                to return your love.
There is a place we have taken together

a place of understanding
a place of love
a place of only
partially that.
I've held my breath
while I've thought of you.
It's only because —
I love you.
You must understand
I carry a right hand
that upsets,
that knocks out all.
You must understand
I'll sit in the Kings' places.
The Queens will ask me.
You must understand
I carry a right arm
that is not gentle.
There is a question
you might ask.
A question about life
silently staying alive.
A question that will
snap a heart-beat
in an instant.
You will have to excuse me
while I kick out the walls
between us.

God struck the first born.
We have learned from the first born
    we are misunderstood
        and we scream
            at the top of our lungs —
    we share
        and we give
            and we give.
Life's blanket of security
    continually gives way
        to death's open arms —
    so we share
        and we share.
Bless God's
    kind heart.
But blindness
    deaf ears
        and cruelty
            grates my teeth.
I have to share with those I love.
I have to give to conclude my destiny.
I must
    to gain a firm hand
        on this quicksand.
You are not alone
    in front of your home
        and I must tell you —
            I love you.

An empty bed
      stared at me.
The sheets were clean
      and nothing had ruffled
            the pillows.
Softly it asked me
      about me.
Softly it beckoned
      to fill me.
An empty bed
      called out to me
            and demanded
                  that I listen.

Quietness seeped
      from the walls.
The radio blasted
      and CNN was sharing the news.
Quietness spread
      through the floors.
Quietness echoed
      through the bedrooms
            the attic and the downstairs.
Quietness screamed at me
      sang to me
            and watched the movie.
The absolute silence
      that haunted me
            before I met you.

Always we shall encounter
        the multi-dimensional existence
                of love.
The anxiousness to give
        and the wonderment
                of receiving from another.
The acceptance
        offers challenges
                enormously different
                        than the giving
Every situation
        offers the continual acceptance
                of balancing and integrating
                        of strengthening our capacity
                                to give and receive.
We don't make the rules.
Life itself has made the rules.
Every situation breathes
        through these rules.
My very existence
        asks me to accept
                these statements,
                        these series of challenges,
                                this recognition.
Love will always seek you
        the very people it needs
                to show that there is
                        compassion and truth,
                kindness and healing hearts
                        breathing its own existence.

169

Those souls
    who absorb and transmute
        the bitterness of disappointment
            offering hope
                to those unable.

All life
    will become a memory
        a place where lessons
            never came easy.
A place the auction block
    bargained
        to buy and sell
            our souls.
The bastards bargained
    never realizing
        they were not
            for sale.
A new place awaits you
    where the ocean breeze
        only recognizes
            your pure heart.
But the lessons will continue
    the lessons remind us
        we are still alive.
There are times
    the miles remind me
        how far we are apart.
But there isn't a time

when I feel
    the miles
        stop the love we share.
We all seek
    a place of refuge.
We all lay awake
    'till it is found.
And the heartbeat we rest next to
    is our own.

Bring An Angel
Into the Life
of Someone You Love.

❧

Additional copies of AN ANGEL CAME
may be ordered through OutBack Insides
Publishing:

~ *$11 per copy.*

~ *Plus $2 shipping and handling on single
orders ($3 on two or more copies).*

~ *Washington state residents please add sales tax.*

❧

┌─ *Please send all orders to:* ─────┐

OutBack Insides Publishing
P. O. Box 1522
Walla Walla, WA 99362

└────────────────────────────┘

*A portion of the proceeds will be lovingly
donated to SAVE THE CHILDREN.*